*leap* THROUGH TIME

# Earthquake

First published in 2004 by Orpheus Books Ltd, 2 Church Green, Witney, Oxon OX28 4AW

Created and produced by Nicholas Harris, Claire Aston and Emma Godfrey, Orpheus Books Ltd

**Text** Nicholas Harris

**Illustrator** Peter Dennis (*Linda Rogers Associates*)

**Consultant** Susanna van Rose, writer and geologist

ISBN 1 901323 80 3

Printed and bound in Malaysia

# leap THROUGH TIME

# Earthquake

*illustrated by*

Peter David Scott

Orpheus

# Contents

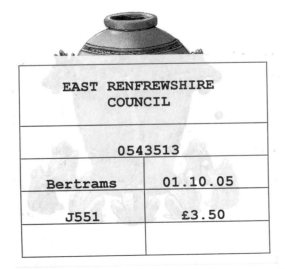

# Introduction

Imagine you are walking along a street in Japan. Suddenly, there is great roar and the ground starts to shake violently beneath your feet. You are in great danger! For the next few minutes, many things happen around you, following on one after the other with frightening speed ...

The story told in this book is like a journey. It is not a journey you can make by plane, car or ship. In fact, you don't have to go anywhere at all. You are about to travel through *time*. With each turn of the page, the time moves forward a few seconds, hours or even years. Each new time—each stop on your journey—is like a chapter in the story. The first violent shaking, the toppling of buildings, the cracks opening up in the ground, the collapse of bridges, the landslide, the vast waves engulfing the shore, the fires sweeping through the devastated city, the rescue of survivors from beneath the rubble, the building of a museum years later to record the events of those fateful moments—all tell the story of the great earthquake.

*Look out for the dog. It is a shikoku, a Japanese breed. It appears in all of the illustrations, although it is not always easy to spot.*

Use this thumb index to travel through time! Just find the page you want to see and flip it open. This way you can make a quick comparison between one scene and another, even though some show events that took place many years apart. A little black arrow on the page points to the time of the scene illustrated on that page.

# About 3000 years ago ...

It is late afternoon on the island of Honshu, Japan. A small band of hunters are returning to their village along the coast path. As they start to climb down through the woods, they are startled by a sudden loud, thundering noise.

Looking up, they see the cliff on the opposite side of the bay collapse into the sea. Out in the water, they see waves start to rear up several metres high and crash on to the shore. Their village, built on the flat land close to the water's edge, will certainly be flooded. It is a horrifying sight.

The men know that an earthquake has struck. This is not an unusual event—small ground tremors lasting a few moments occur almost weekly—but no damage or injury is caused. This quake is different. The men have never seen so much of the cliff collapse before, nor witnessed such colossal waves ...

## WHAT IS AN EARTHQUAKE?

The outer layer of the Earth is made up of a number of giant slabs, called *tectonic plates*. These are always on the move. In some places, the edges are moving apart. In others they are colliding, with one plate sliding underneath the other. In still others, one plate edge slides alongside another plate. This movement is very slow—about 1cm a year—but the pressure is enormous. When plate edges grind against one another, they send out shock waves through the ground. We feel these as the vibrations which are earthquakes.

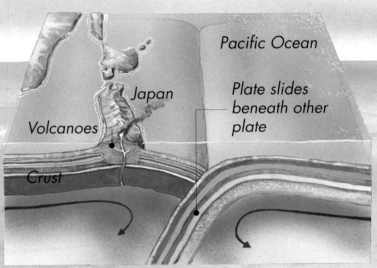

*Pacific Ocean*

*Japan*

*Plate slides beneath other plate*

Volcanoes

*Crust*

Most earthquakes are small tremors that do no damage. But when sliding plates "lock" together, pressure builds up in the rocks underground. Eventually the pressure becomes too much for the rock to withstand. It snaps, causing a major earthquake.

The place where the rock breaks is called the *focus* of the earthquake. The point above it on the Earth's surface is termed the *epicentre*.

Japan suffers from many earthquakes because it is situated near plate boundaries. The Pacific plate is sliding down beneath the Eurasian plate.

# A hundred years ago ...

The village has grown over the years and has now become a prosperous city with a busy sea port. The streets are crowded with carts and rickshaws. Street sellers offer all kinds of things for sale, including food, clothing, clogs, lanterns and toys. Amid all the noise and bustle, a funeral procession slowly winds its way through the crowds. In one of the buildings, a tea ceremony is being held.

Area of landslide

Funeral procession

Lamps

Lanterns

Rickshaw

8

Over the years, the city has suffered many earthquakes. Most have been far too weak for anybody to notice, although some stronger quakes have caused some minor damage. The city's buildings have been constructed in a particular way, which makes them very resistant to earthquake shaking. Walls are made of wood and, between rooms inside the houses, with paper. The wooden beams holding up the thatch roofs are tied with rice straw ropes.

1000 BC

100 years ago

Part of roof cut away

Tea ceremony

Toys

Clogs

Smoked fish

9

Thousands of earth-quakes occur every year, some of them major ones. But only where cities are affected is there great loss of life.

# A few years ago ...

The city is a modern metropolis. Many of its traditional buildings have been demolished and replaced by multistorey blocks, built of steel and glass.

This morning the weather is unusually hot and humid. The fog

Inside apartment

rolling in from the sea has been slow to lift. Cars and buses take people to work along the city streets as usual, but today there is a strange feeling in the air. Animals, including sea birds and people's pet dogs, are restless and jumpy. Some fishermen stand about and chat on the pavement. Unusually, they have caught no fish at all that morning. Many report having seen strange lights in the sea fog earlier. One old man, who remembers witnessing very similar events many years ago, is in no doubt as to what all this means. He tells whoever will listen: there will be an earthquake soon.

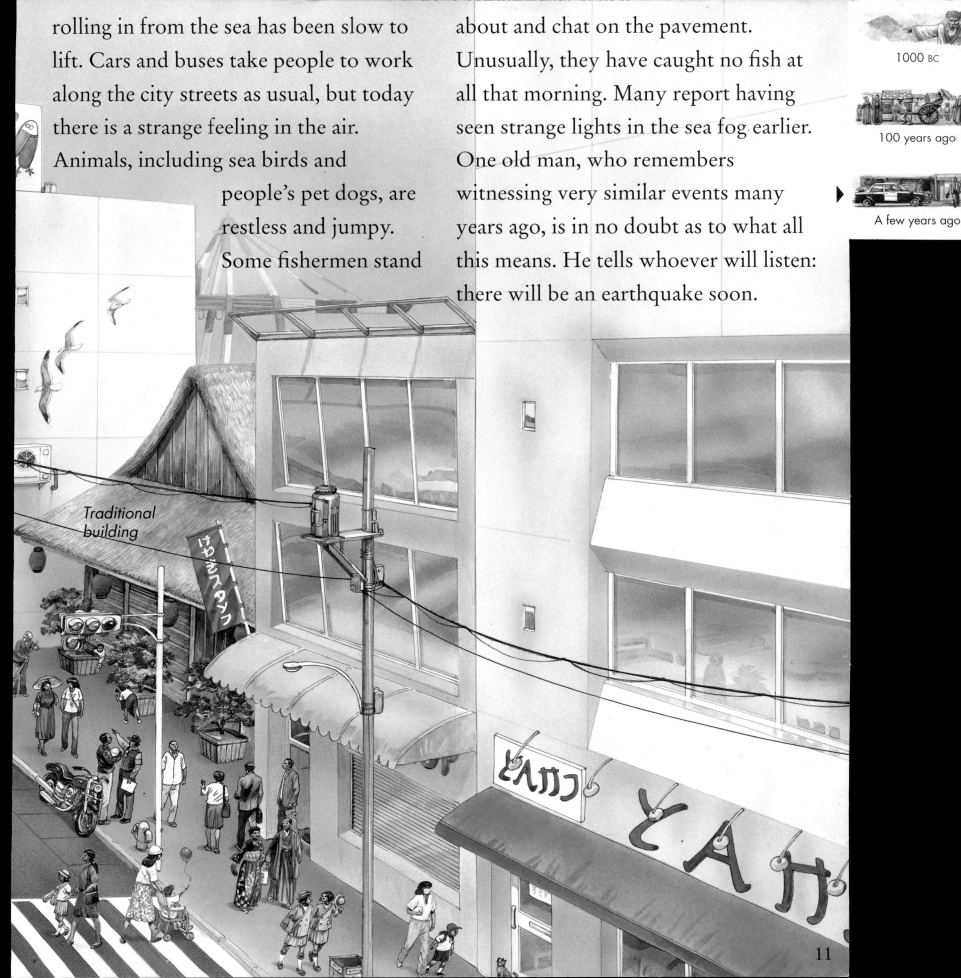

Traditional building

1000 BC

100 years ago

A few years ago

11

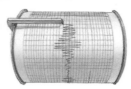

Later that day ...

The old man is right. An earthquake strikes that very afternoon.

With a deafening roar, the whole city starts to shake violently. Within seconds, large concrete slabs start to fall off the outsides of buildings

Burst pipe

and crash to the ground. Glass panes fall and shatter on the pavements below. In some buildings, the walls fall outwards, causing the concrete floors to collapse on top of one another like a pack of cards. Sirens wail amid the din of falling rubble.

People dash out into the street, screaming in panic. As they do so, great cracks in the road's surface start to open up. Cars swerve to avoid the cracks and screech to a halt. Some collide with each other, or smash into buildings. Water from burst pipes and underground drains pours out on to the streets. Electricity cables spark and crackle.

Everywhere, there is chaos.

1000 BC

100 years ago

A few years ago

Later that day

Collapsing building

Crack

# Seconds later ...

Inside an apartment, a family just sitting down to a meal find themselves being hurled around their kitchen. The rocking and juddering causes plates to tip out of cupboards, pots and pans to crash to the floor and even the furniture and electrical appliances to slide around the room. Cracks appear in the ceiling and lumps of plaster start to crash down amid clouds of dust.

The children scream. Their mother shouts to them to get under the table. Everyone is terrfied. It feels like a sickening roller-coaster ride where everything is breaking up around them.

## UNSTABLE GROUND

When shock waves from an earthquake pass through solid rock, it is completely unaffected. But shock waves passing through sediments such as moist sand or gravel cause them to become almost like a liquid. This is called *liquefaction*. Buildings sink into the liquefied sediments and topple over. Mexico City was built on old lake sediments, so many buildings were badly damaged when an earthquake struck the region in 1985. The districts of San Francisco that were damaged in the 1989 quake had been built on top of debris from the 1906 earthquake that had been dumped in the waterfront area.

1000 BC

100 years ago

A few years ago

Later that day

Seconds later

15

When rocks snap, two kinds of shock waves are released from the earthquake's focus. Primary (P) waves *(above)* squeeze and stretch the rocks. Secondary (S) waves *(below)* shake them up and down and from side to side.

# At the same time ...

Just outside the city, farmers in the ricefields are flung to the ground by the force of the earthquake. To the alarm of the terrified onlookers, the land itself rises and falls like the surface of the ocean as waves surge across it. In the fields, fountains of mud spurt into the air like miniature volcanoes. Cracks appear in the field and a nearby road buckles, throwing cars off the edge.

Shock waves

Mud fountains

With a deafening crack, a railway bridge suddenly give way as its concrete supports collapse. The tracks start to slump. The train driver slams on his brakes in a desperate attempt to stop his train from plunging to the ground.

## FAULTS

Rocks can bend and fold without breaking. Sometimes, when subjected to great pressure, they may suddenly break. The crack in the rocks where this sudden movement takes place is called a *fault*. As the pressure continues, rocks may move past one another along the same fault. During an earthquake, portions of land may be raised up or slip down along fault lines.

1000 BC

100 years ago

A few years ago

Later that day

Seconds later

At the same time

*Elevated railway*

17

These globes show where earthquakes occur around the world. Most take place at or near plate boundaries *(see page 7)*. The biggest are where plate edges slide alongside, or where one slides under another.

# A few minutes later ...

After 20 seconds the quake is over. But the violent shuddering of the ground has not only caused buildings to collapse. Up on a hillside overlooking the city, the rocks and soil just beneath the surface have been made unstable by recent heavy rain. Now, triggered by the quake, the slope itself gives way. In a gigantic landslide, tonnes of boulders and soil, together with trees and shrubs, start to surge downhill. Houses, cars and anything else in the way of the landslide are carried along with it, so adding to the slide. Alerted by the thunderous noise of falling rocks, people dash from their houses and flee for their lives ...

1000 BC

100 years ago

A few years ago

Later that day

Seconds later

At the same time

A few minutes later

19

The San Andreas Fault stretches more than 1200 km along the coast of California. It forms the boundary between two plates that are sliding past one another in opposite directions. The jerky movements result in constant, tiny shocks. Occasionally, pressure builds up over the years and is released in a massive quake, such as the 1906 event in San Francisco.

Rescuing survivors

Finding survivors

Ambulance

# Twenty minutes later ...

During the quake, some people did not have time to escape before the buildings they were in collapsed. Miraculously, a few strong beams held up parts of the building in this street and saved people from being totally crushed. But they are now buried beneath piles of rubble. They have only dusty air to breathe and there is a risk that an aftershock (a lesser tremor that takes place after the main quake) will destroy their fragile shelter. They cry out, hoping someone will rescue them quickly.

Soon, a crowd of helpers, including firemen, emergency medical teams and some brave people who did manage to escape the falling buildings, rush to the scene. Listening out for shouts of help, they lift away the rubble and cut through wood and twisted metal. Eventually a loud cheer goes up as the first survivors are hauled to safety. They are carefully stretchered over the rubble to a waiting ambulance.

Just then, an aftershock causes the remains of the building to collapse. The rescuers were just in time!

1000 BC

100 years ago

A few years ago

Later that day

Seconds later

At the same time

A few minutes later

20 minutes later

When the epicentre of an earthquake is on the sea bed, a large submarine landslide can result *(above)*. This produces a series of fast moving waves, travelling at around 800 km per hour, called tsunamis (also sometimes known as tidal waves). In deep water, they are small, but as they approach the shallow coastal waters they slow down and build up in height. Some tsunamis are tens of metres high as they crash on to the shore *(below)*. The waves may last for several hours.

# A few minutes later ...

On the sea front, a group of people suddenly notice a massive wave out to sea, getting bigger all the time and rapidly moving towards them.

"Tsunami!" they yell, and everybody runs for their lives.

Soon, a wall of water some 30 metres high looms into view. Ships and boats of all sizes are picked up and, as the giant wave surges across the docks, are hurled

on to the shore. Many more tsunami follow, one after the other, over the next few hours. A hotel building on the sea front escapes destruction by allowing the torrents of water to pass unhindered through its lower floors.

## TSUNAMIS

*Tsunami* is a Japanese word meaning "a wave breaking into a harbour". Most tsunamis are caused by earthquakes on the sea bed. Some, triggered by quakes in one part of the world, do great damage to coastal areas in another part a long way away. The great Chilean earthquake of May 1960 created tsunamis that devastated Japan 16,000 km away.

1000 BC

100 years ago

A few years ago

Later that day

Seconds later

At the same time

A few minutes later

20 minutes later

A few minutes later

The Mercalli Scale records the intensity of damage caused by an earthquake.
I-IV Felt only by a few.
III-IV Vibration as if by passing lorry.

V Buildings tremble, vases fall, trees shake.
VI Bells ring, plaster cracks, people shaken.
VII Loose tiles, old walls fall, chimneys crack.

VIII Damage to buildings.
IX Ground cracks, buildings collapse.
X Landslides, bridges damaged, rails bent.
XI Dams wrecked.
XII Total devastation.

# Several hours later ...

Night has fallen, but the effects of the earthquake are far from over. Fire has broken out in the city. Sparked by fallen power lines and fed by gas escaping from

broken gas pipes, the flames quickly fan out among the stricken city's buildings. Moreover, broken water pipes make it very difficult for the firemen to put out the fires. Here they are using a pump to bring in water from other parts of the city where pipes are still intact. Elsewhere, they will need to blow up some buildings to stop the fire from spreading.

People who have been rescued from fallen buildings sit together in the street as the teams of firefighters attempt to save their homes from even further destruction. Meanwhile, rescue workers continue their search for survivors. They still have hopes that more people can be brought out from under the rubble. They will work on through the night.

1000 BC

100 years ago

A few years ago

Later that day

Seconds later

At the same time

A few minutes later

20 minutes later

A few minutes later

Several hours later

Traditional building

25

The Transamerica Building in San Francisco is specially designed to withstand even the most severe earthquakes. It is shaped like a slender pyramid and, thanks to special steel supports, its top is strong enough to sway 12 m and still remain intact. In 1989 an earthquake shook California. Its epicentre was 100 km south of San Francisco. Although quite severe, the quake damaged few buildings in San Francisco. Most had been built to resist earthquake shaking.

# The next morning ...

Dawn breaks on a scene of utter devastation. A reporter flies over the city in a helicopter, relaying to his shocked radio listeners what he can see below. Many buildings are damaged or totally destroyed. Large sections of the elevated roadway have collapsed. Fire and flooding have ravaged much of the city.

*Helicopter*

*Collapsed buildings*

*Collapsed roadway*

But the story is not wholly gloomy. Many buildings, specially built to withstand earthquakes, have remained undamaged. They include a number of old buildings, with their wooden or paper walls and thatched roofs. And, despite the great ferocity of the quake, most of the city's inhabitants escaped harm. They have spent the night sleeping in tents. For the next few weeks, they will be without electricity and running water, but at least they are alive.

Fire-damaged buildings

Toppled building

Tents

1000 BC

100 years ago

A few years ago

Later that day

Seconds later

At the same time

A few minutes later

20 minutes later

A few minutes later

Several hours later

The next morning

There are several ways in which buildings can be constructed to withstand severe quakes. Walls are anchored to concrete foundations reinforced with steel rods *(above)*.

Steel brackets anchor brick chimneys to the roof. Metal chimneys are lighter and safer.

Boilers are held in place by straps bolted to the wall, preventing gas pipes from breaking.

Steel connectors reinforce the joins between the wooden beams and joists supporting the floors and ceilings.

Video

Globe showing where earthquakes occur

Model of traditional house

Model of city struck by earthquake

Seismograph

# Today, a few years later

A party of schoolchildren are visiting a museum. It was built recently as a record of the terrible events of a few years ago, in which the city suffered its worst-ever earthquake.

The exhibits tell people all about earthquakes. There are models showing the Earth's plates and what a fault in the rocks looks like. The visitors watch a video of what happened during the quake in their city, and gaze at a model of the immense damage it caused.

There are also exhibits that show how traditional houses were built to withstand earthquakes. A seismograph records small tremors as they actually happen in the city today.

Children have a go on an earthquake simulator. The floor shakes around, making it very difficult for them to stand upright. The children have a lot of fun falling about, but their parents remember that when the real earthquake struck, the shaking was so violent they feared for their lives.

Rebuilt city

Model of fault

Earthquake simulator

1000 BC

100 years ago

A few years ago

Later that day

Seconds later

At the same time

A few minutes later

20 minutes later

A few minutes later

Several hours later

The next morning

Today

# Glossary

**Aftershock** A lesser tremor that takes place after the main earthquake. There may be many aftershocks, sometimes continuing for months afterwards.

**Crust** The thin, rocky outer layer of the Earth.

**Earthquake** A shaking of the ground caused by the sudden movement of part of the Earth's crust. Earthquakes usually (but not always) occur at or near the boundaries of tectonic plates.

**Epicentre** The point on the Earth's surface directly above the focus of an earthquake.

**Fault** A crack in the Earth's surface produced when pressure from plate movements causes brittle rocks to break. The rocks move in opposite directions on either side of the fault, causing an earthquake.

**Focus** The point in the Earth's crust where the rocks suddenly break, releasing shock waves.

**Foundations** The base of a building constructed so that its weight is supported on firm ground or bedrock.

**Landslide** The sudden and rapid movement of soil and rock down a slope.

**Liquefaction** The process by which moist sediments, when shock waves are passed through them, become almost like a liquid.

**Mercalli Scale** A measure of the intensity of damage caused by earthquake shaking, based on the effects on buildings and the landscape.

**P(rimary) wave** A shock wave released from the focus of an earthquake. P-waves cause the rocks to shake back and forth in the direction of wave movement.

**Richter Scale** A measure of the magnitude (size or strength) of an earthquake. An increase of 1 point means that an earthquake is 30 times stronger. On the Richter Scale an earthquake with a magnitude of less than 4 is described as minor; 4-5 is light; 5-6 is moderate; 6-7 is strong; 7-8 is major; 8-9 is great.

**S(econdary) wave** A shock wave released from the focus of an earthquake. S-waves cause the rocks to shake from side to side and up and down at right angles to the direction of wave movement.

**Sediments** Eroded rock fragments, such as sand and gravel, transported and laid down by wind, water or ice, usually in layers.

**Seismograph** A device that makes a permanent record of earthquake shaking.

**Seismometer** An instrument for measuring movements in the Earth's crust.

**Shock wave** A wave of energy released from the focus of an earthquake. Also called a seismic wave.

**Tectonic plates** The large slabs into which the Earth's surface is divided. Each plate moves slowly, either pushing into another plate, pulling away from it, or sliding underneath it.

**Tremor** A shaking of the ground.

**Tsunami** A sea wave caused by an earthquake occurring beneath the sea bed.

# Index